Technology in the Music Class

ROBERT A. CARPENTER

Alfred Publishing Co., Inc.
Los Angeles

NOV - 5 '97

Publisher: Morton Manus
Editor in Chief: John O'Reilly
Managing Editor: Patrick Wilson
Acquisition/Project Editor: Dave Black
Production Editor: Bruce Frausto
Interior Photos: Cathryn Scott
Cover Design: Ted Engelbart/Greg McKinney
Cover Photo: CRISP microprocessor (detail), courtesy of AT&T
    Bell Laboratories and the Museum of Modern Art, New York

Alfred Publishing Co., Inc.
16380 Roscoe Blvd., Suite 200
Van Nuys, CA 91406

ISBN 0-88284-493-8

CONTENTS

INTRODUCTION

In order to be successful, music teachers must develop an enormous number of personal and professional skills over the course of their careers. They must be accomplished musicians, master teachers, motivators, recruiters and public relations experts. They often master the complexities of student schedules in order to meet with performing groups. They become experts in the technical as well as artistic aspects of musical rehearsal and performance, and are flexible enough to perform under the most rigorous of conditions.

Yet with all of this complexity in their everyday world, music teachers frequently have little or no confidence in their ability to work successfully with technology in their classrooms. There may be several reasons for this. Teachers may feel that technology is too complex for them to learn. After all, they majored in music, not engineering or computer programming, and they don't understand how the "insides" of these things actually work. These same individuals have been creating and producing photocopies for years without having any idea of the inner workings of a copy machine or what the horsepower rating of the machine's motor might be. The insides of these machines are a mystery, but most teachers make extensive use of this technology with confidence.

Another reason for a lack of technological confidence may be that teachers aren't sure how technology could make a contribution in their classrooms. In other words, they aren't convinced of the value of new technology and are hesitant to invest the resources to purchase it or the time necessary to master it. This is particularly true when initially learning a new technology, since it's frequently more difficult and more time-consuming to produce a product at first. Some marching band directors have observed that they can produce a set of charts for formations and drills faster by hand than by using a computer-based charting program. Although this may be true initially, their proficiency would increase with practice, and other benefits, such as ease of editing to match music cuts may become apparent in the process. This sense of insecurity about the real value of a new approach is experienced by many teachers when confronting a new teaching technique or approach for which the they feel unprepared. If a teacher is unfamiliar with the concepts underlying the Orff approach to teaching music, it's likely that he or she won't have a full understanding of the benefits that Orff techniques can bring to their classroom.

Music teachers nationwide are investigating the contributions technology might make to the lives of their students. These teachers range from beginners to veterans nearing the end of their careers. They seem to share a common goal of wanting to retain those values and techniques that have always characterized good teaching while discovering the legitimate role that technology can serve in improving the educational experience of their students. Most people today see the limitations of technology, and fewer and fewer teachers harbor fears of being replaced by machines. A more realistic concern is that musicians and music teachers will ignore technology and choose to let others control the direction that the use of these tools might take in the music classroom. Music teachers should be the professionals who determine what technology is used and how it is used in their classrooms. If they choose to ignore this role, then manufacturers, software developers and technology specialists will certainly attempt to fill the void that they leave.

This book is meant to provide a source of basic information concerning the technology that is available, its capabilities and its potential uses in the teaching of music. For those needing more detailed information about equipment, owner's manuals and manufacturers' catalogs are good sources to consult. There are also several magazines that focus on music technology. These include *Keyboard, Electronic Musician* and *The Music and Computer Educator*.

Every teacher's use of technology will be tailored to his or her own situation. Those individuals with a vision of how technology might be used in their classroom should pursue that goal. There are no limits or conditions that need be imposed on the use of technology in music instruction. Every example provided is taken from the experience of practicing classroom music teachers. Most started with no formal training in technology and have found their way through the maze of wires and disks to use computers and synthesizers successfully in their classrooms.

1

AUDIO EQUIPMENT

Audio equipment is the critical link between electronic sound sources and our ears. Audio equipment makes it possible for us actually to hear the sounds created in an electronic medium. This equipment also enables us to alter the sound and fine tune it to our preferences. Audio systems can include mixers, equalizers, effects units, monitor systems, amplifiers and speakers, and tape recorders. The function of each piece of audio equipment and its relationship to other units can be seen in the flow of audio signals through the system.

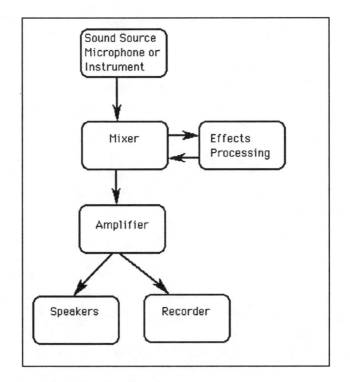

Mixers contain several input channels, each capable of receiving an audio signal; these signals are blended for balance to create a mix. Each channel has the same set of controls. Usually a mixer channel contains several sections of controls, each having a specific function. Following the path of the audio signal (top to bottom in the diagram) these controls include the following:

1. Input-level controls ensure that the incoming signal is strong enough without being distorted.

2. Equalization or tone controls allow the user to adjust the relative prominence of specific frequencies. Since the human ear is more sensitive to certain frequency ranges than others these controls can have a significant effect on the final sound.

3. There are usually multiple sets of auxiliary send/return controls, pan/buss switches and input faders. One set enables the user to send a certain amount of audio signal to some device that can add various effects. Reverb, chorusing or other effects can be added and the signal returned to the mix. These effects make it possible to create a more realistic sound and use electronics to duplicate the conditions found in natural acoustic settings, e.g., various-sized concert halls, rooms, or nightclubs.

Another set of send/return controls is used to create the *monitor mix*, which is a mix of the signals that can be customized for a performer. This can serve several purposes. A performer might want to hear more or less of a particular part, or he or she might prefer to hear the piano to the left and the bass and drums to the right. Perhaps a singer would like to hear the lead line and the piano more prominently than the bass and background singers. This can be accomplished by adjusting the send control for the parts desired and amplifying or panning them for the performer.

4. The *pan* (short for panorama) control positions an audio signal in the left-right stereo field. Panning is critical in creating the illusion of space and distance in a mix.

5. Each channel has a fader which controls the amount of signal added into the final mix. The faders are moved during the final mix process in order to achieve the desired balance.

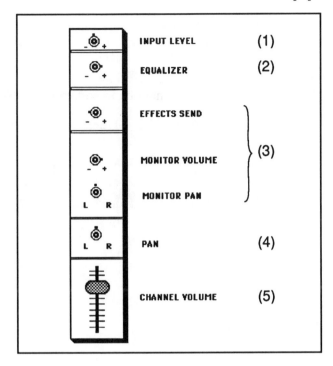

INPUT LEVEL	(1)
EQUALIZER	(2)
EFFECTS SEND	
MONITOR VOLUME	(3)
MONITOR PAN	
PAN	(4)
CHANNEL VOLUME	(5)

Finally, the fine-tuned sound is sent to an amplifier and then to a set of speakers and/or a tape recorder. An amplifier's purpose is to increase the volume of the sound. They are available in mono or stereo, and it is up to the individual to decide which is best suited for his or her situation.

Tape recorders are available with many different features. For more sophisticated projects, a multi-track recorder might be most useful. With this type of recorder, a performer can record one track, then rewind the tape and record another track while listening to the original. Students might create their own radio-type commercials by recording their voice on one track, music on another and sound effects on a third.

Classroom Uses

One of the most obvious classroom applications of this technology is as a bridge between traditional music vocabulary and electronic vocabulary identifying the same musical concept. Although vocabulary is important, the real goal is that the student hear the difference in the music indicated by the word or symbol. For example, a student can be asked to use a volume control on the mixer to change the loudness of a particular sound based on a piece of printed music. As the dynamics change from piano to mezzo-piano to forte, the student should respond by increasing the volume of the channel he or she is controlling. Several students can control several channels and respond to the blend and balance demanded by the music.

Students can manipulate the various controls on the mixer and understand what effect the changes they make actually have on the sound. They may use their own words to describe the sound.

2

MIDI BASICS

MIDI stands for Musical Instrument Digital Interface. MIDI standardizes digital communication of musical messages. Prior to MIDI's implementation, synthesizers from different manufacturers couldn't communicate with one another. This standard initially allowed one musical instrument to trigger sounds in another instrument. If one instrument was set to the sound of a piano and was connected via MIDI to another set to strings, then by playing the first instrument a blended piano/strings sound could be produced. Since the messages that are transmitted are digital in nature, their content is expressed in numerical form.

Students learn the use of a mixing console one component at a time.

As the MIDI standard developed, engineers found other musical messages that could be expressed in numerical terms. At this point, several kinds of messages are available. These are summarized in the following table:

Message	Content
Note on	Causes a note to begin sounding.
Note off	Causes a note to stop. Must follow a Note message or else the sound will sustain indefinitely.
Note number	Designates the pitch to be sounded. Middle C is note number 60, C# is note number 61, etc.
Patch/Program	Selects which of 128 available patches should be used.
Velocity	Can be used to control the strength of individual notes.
Pitch bend	Raises or lowers pitch.
Modulation	Causes a modulation of the sound similar to vibrato. Depth and frequency can be set.

As trained musicians, we have all learned to interpret a system of notation that is supposed to describe visually what we hear with our ears. This system contains symbols that have meaning for the trained eye. There are rules that govern the interpretation of these symbols, but it is possible for musicians to understand other systems of notation that seem to describe the same events. Roman numerals describe chords in one notation system, while another system uses letter names and numbers for extensions. Understanding MIDI messages is much the same process.

There is a great deal of precision available through MIDI. Just as a traditional performer might wish to interpret the length of a quarter note for the sake of style or expressiveness, so can MIDI performers exercise the same type of exactitude. Quarter notes are divided into units, called ticks. A quarter note may be divided into 48, 96, or 480 ticks, depending on the software. If a quarter note receives 480 ticks, then a legato quarter note might be 460 ticks, while a staccato quarter note might be 320 ticks. All other rhythmic values can be expressed in some number of beats and ticks. Some software programs divide a quarter note into 1,256 ticks for even greater *resolution* (ability to define duration) and flexibility.

Here is a list of terms musicians might use to describe musical events, along with terms that might be used to describe the same events as MIDI messages.

Musician	MIDI
Note attack	Note on
Note release	Note off
Middle C	Note number
Quarter note	480 ticks
Eighth note	240 ticks
Whole note	960 ticks
pp	Velocity= 30
mf	Velocity= 64
ff	Velocity=127

From these individual examples of specific events it is possible to look at a musical line as comprising one MIDI event after another. Here are two versions of the same musical idea. Both would sound the same and would convey the same information.

MIDI Messages

Time	Note	Velocity	Duration
1|1|000	D Major		
	4/4	click ♩	
	♪A3	↓64 ↑64	1|000
1|2|000	♪G3	↓64 ↑64	0|240
1|2|240	♪F#3	↓64 ↑64	0|240
1|3|000	♪D3	↓64 ↑64	2|000
2|2|000	♪E3	↓64 ↑64	1|000
2|3|000	♪D3	↓64 ↑64	2|000
3|1|000	♪A3	↓64 ↑64	0|240
3|1|240	♪G3	↓64 ↑64	0|240
3|2|000	♪F#3	↓64 ↑64	0|240
3|2|240	♪G3	↓64 ↑64	0|240
3|3|000	♪A3	↓64 ↑64	2|000
4|1|000	♪D3	↓64 ↑64	4|000

Traditional Notation

As part of the development of the MIDI standard, it was decided to include 16 available channels that could be used to transmit or receive information. This ability to "channelize" information makes it possible to send independent musical lines to a number of instruments with different timbres. *Sequencers* use this feature to send *tracks* containing musical information to a destination such as a synthesizer or drum machine. The track window below shows how information is sent to devices that are set to receive information on a particular channel. The Roland D50 will receive the flute part on channel 1, while the Proteus will receive the bass part on channel 8.

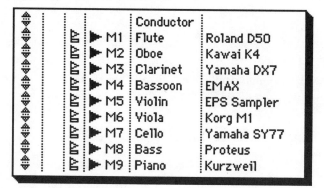

Classroom Uses

Some students struggle to understand many of the basic musical concepts that are important in the appreciation of music. These concepts are sometimes too abstract to learn from just listening to a variety of examples. If students can actually "play around" with music and change the way it sounds, they can gain a more personalized understanding of the elements of music. For example, as students use MIDI technology to increase or decrease volume, they are actually causing and controlling crescendo and decrescendo. Since style in music is often a function of articulation, tempo and volume, students can manipulate style with the movement of a wheel.

Hardware- and software-based sequencers can be used to capture MIDI events and then play these events back through a sound source such as a synthesizer or sampler. Students can record their own improvisations, edit them and then make cassette recordings that they can listen to at home. The most unique feature of using a sequencer in a classroom is that the performance of the student can be suspended in time while subtle changes are made. This is unique to the realm of electronics, since it cannot be duplicated on tape or in live performance.

Audio equipment can be used for a variety of purposes in the technology studio, including ear training, self-evaluation from recording and as a reference tool for ideas.

3

SYNTHESIZERS/ KEYBOARDS/SAMPLERS

Electronic keyboards, synthesizers and samplers all serve as sound sources in the electronic music world. **Electronic keyboards** usually contain only a few sounds stored in memory, which are simply selected one at a time. *Synthesizers* use a variety of techniques to generate sound synthetically using electricity. These instruments usually have more sounds available than keyboards do, and these sounds are usually more complex and sophisticated. *Samplers* can digitally record acoustic sounds and manipulate these sounds in interesting ways.

Electronic keyboard instruments are the least expensive and contain the fewest number of available timbres of the available sound sources. The sounds in these instruments cannot be edited or fine tuned to suit the tastes of the user. Some instruments contain rhythm units that produce a variety of drum patterns to keep time and provide a particular "feel" for the music. The user can choose "swing, "rock, "samba" or another style, select a tempo for the pattern, and push the start/begin button to start the *looped* pattern. Some units contain a limited, self-contained *sequencer* that will record and play back musical ideas programmed by the user in real time. These sequencers usually lack sophisticated editing capabilities. *Effects* processing such as reverb or chorusing may be available on some machines to enhance the sound.

Different manufacturers have chosen to implement synthesis in a variety of ways. These methods might include any number of traditional or proprietary methods of synthesis, or a combination of methods. Synthesizers often contain 128 or more accessible sounds, which can be selected instantly by the push of a button or turn of a wheel. In addition to the sounds stored in the internal memory of the instrument, many models utilize expansion cartridges or cards that can store additional sounds providing the user with a much wider array of available sounds. The sounds stored in synthesizers can be edited or "tweaked" until they are customized to the user's satisfaction. This means that each of the parameters necessary to define a sound can be adjusted within a range of values. Completely new sounds can be created by design or randomly by simply changing the various parameters until a new, interesting timbre is produced.

Samplers usually utilize a disk drive to load sounds into memory, rather than storing them permanently on board. In addition, sounds can be fed into samplers through either a microphone or a line from a source such as a cassette player, CD player or VCR. These sounds are sampled i.e., digitally recorded, and the sound data can subsequently be manipulated and stored to disk. These instruments are probably the most capable of recreating the sounds of acoustic instruments since they are actually playing back recordings of the original sounds.

The wide range of sampler prices can be attributed to variation in the amount of memory and the processing power provided on different models. The longer a sample lasts, and the greater its *frequency* range, the larger it becomes, and the more memory is required to store all of its data. This additional memory capability adds cost to a unit. The *sampling rate* of the unit determines the frequency range of the samples it produces. A higher sampling rate produces samples with greater audiofidelity. However, these more lifelike samples require greater amounts of memory for storage, which in turn drives up the cost of the sampler. Most samplers attempt to maximize memory use by allowing the user to record and play back samples at a variety of sampling rates depending on the frequency range of the source sound. In general, low sounds such as a bass drum or bass guitar don't need the extended range of, say, a violin or flute. These can be processed at a lower rate, perhaps half the full rate of the sampler, and will require less memory for storage. Quite acceptable results can be obtained in processing many instruments at reduced sampling rates.

Many of the sound sources available in keyboard form are also available in smaller, rack-mountable versions designed to fit into 19-inch equipment racks. These units generally contain the same electronics housed in the keyboard models, but are usually smaller and less expensive because the keyboard is omitted. However, in many cases schools will have multiple keyboard players and will see a real need in having a full set of keys attached to each of their sound sources.

An alternative that is becoming more widespread is the creation of expansion cards or chips that contain sounds and that can simply be installed in a computer. This allows the computer to function as a sampler or synthesizer that can be triggered just as if it were a separate keyboard instrument.

Classroom Uses

Music ensembles often find themselves short on particular instruments. Schools also always seem to have a number of students who have had some piano instruction, either privately or in a group. These students can make a contribution to the ensemble by performing a missing part using a synthesizer. Bass parts can be reinforced when needed, and the synthesizer will provide a steady pitch center for other musicians. Student musicians or computers can control these sound sources to provide solo accompaniment or give support to a small orchestra working to prepare a score for Broadway-type musical performance.

Many music software programs support the use of MIDI-equipped keyboards as input devices. For example, these instruments can be used to identify pitches on a staff or as the source of interval data in theory programs. Even the most basic MIDI keyboard can perform this function.

Technology studios can have a variety of configurations depending on the purpose and the available space.

A synthesizer can be a wonderful learning tool for students to gain a better understanding of sound and acoustics. Some children are thrilled at the possibility of creating a new, never-before-heard synthesizer sound.

Samplers can be used to capture everyday sounds that can then be used in musical settings. A thunderclap might become a bass drum, or a student's name might be used as an ostinato in a simple composition.

In classrooms, students can use these sound sources as raw materials for their creative endeavors. Students can express themselves in new ways using new sounds. They can learn to combine instrumental timbres in both traditional and novel ways. Students enjoy the opportunity to make use of this equipment in creative ways. They accept it as their own tool.

Synthesizer ensembles give students an opportunity to share ideas.

4

DRUM MACHINES

Drum machines are devices that contain a variety of percussion sounds, usually sampled, that can be arranged in rhythmic patterns. These patterns can be further assembled in any order to create songs or longer chains of songs.

Patterns are created by tapping rhythms on a set of pads, with each pad being assigned to a particular percussion timbre. Drum machines can also serve as a source of timing information to synchronize musical events among MIDI devices. Drum machines are frequently used as sources for percussion sounds, since they contain a large variety of quality sounds and can be accessed via MIDI.

Drum machines can vary in several ways. Sounds can be permanently stored in memory or loaded from cards (or other storage devices). The number type and quality of sounds varies significantly from unit to unit. Some units allow users to assemble unique sets of sounds for particular songs or projects. One set of sounds might include a drum kit consisting of a kick drum, a snare drum, various tom-toms and cymbals. Another set might include a group of Latin instruments, and yet another might include a series of Oriental gongs and bells. If the sounds are synthesized, then various parameters of a sound may be altered such as the *attack*, *sustain* or *release*. For example, if the sound of a gong was fine except that it faded away too quickly, then the decay time could be extended.

Many drum machines give the user the choice of creating patterns in *real time* or in *step time*. Writing a pattern in real time means the performer plays the pattern to a metronomic pulse provided by the machine. The sequence of notes played is recorded by the machine and can be stored in memory. This is very much like playing a drum kit or percussion instrument and having the result recorded. A commonly available feature in real-time performance is *quantization* or *auto-*

15

correction, which rounds off the performance of the player so that the notes played are shifted to the nearest sixteenth or nearest thirty-second note. This corrects "out of time" performances, and allows students with limited skills to create patterns that sound good and have a sense of realism.

Step-time writing of patterns involves entering patterns note-by-note (and rest-by-rest). The user must define a rhythmic duration and then choose an instrument or timbre to play that note or rest. The next duration is selected, the instrument chosen, then played. This process is repeated until the pattern is completed. This is particularly useful when the desired pattern is too difficult or the dexterity of the player is not adequate to perform in real time.

Drum machines may respond differently depending on the velocity with which the pads are hit. As the pads are hit progressively harder, the volume of the note may increase or the timbre may change. This quality of responding differently depending on the velocity with which a pad is hit is called *touch sensitivity* or *velocity sensitivity*. In addition to the volume of individual notes, the relative volume of each instrument may be controlled as well as the master volume level of the entire unit.

Finally, drum machines equipped with MIDI technology can serve as a master or slave for the overall timing of musical events. For example, the drum machine's internal clock can be used to control the tempo at which a computer sends musical information to a synthesizer, acting as the master timing generator. It can also receive this same type of information and simply play back stored patterns according to a tempo supplied by a computer. This ability to serve as the master (generate internal clock) or slave (receive external clock) can be very useful depending on the goals set by the musician.

Classroom Uses

Because drum machines allow for such accurate control of rhythms, they make great teaching tools for demonstrating rhythmic concepts. Teachers can create very simple or complex musical examples that students can be asked to listen to and identify particular timbres or patterns. Examples can be generated immediately by the student or teacher and saved for future use with other classes.

With the relative ease of use of these devices, students can create their own rhythmic patterns almost immediately. Their creation can be

Students enjoy creating their own patterns on drum machines.

guided by the teacher who can provide information concerning the ways in which sounds blend or contrast. Students may attempt to create patterns that are too busy or have too little material. The teacher can provide advice concerning the compositions. This allows children to fulfill the basic music education goal of musical creation. Students can achieve success quickly and easily, since the machine can quantize their performance to smooth out any programming errors and allow their compositions to sound like "real" music.

Drum machines can be invaluable in providing a time source for performance groups. They can aid rhythm-section players in improving their time-keeping. Drum machines can be a cost-effective way to add a variety of percussion sounds to the band or choir room. Instead of purchasing a large number of exotic Latin instruments that might be used infrequently, a teacher might opt to purchase a drum machine containing these sounds and simply use it as a performance instrument for rehearsals and concerts. Drum machines can be used by percussionists as sophisticated practice metronomes or as a means to create and test patterns and rhythms that they later incorporate in their playing.

A final consideration might be the use of a drum machine as an introduction to music technology. As a first instrument for instruction, the drum machine offers many advantages. It is simple to operate, and the student can achieve success quickly. It introduces the concept of time represented by both traditional rhythmic values as well as numeric values and allows the student to focus on only the rhythmic aspects of music. It also allows the student to consider the final output of the music and the manipulation of the controls of an amplifier such as volume, tone, and stereo balance.

5

MIDI APPLICATIONS

Alternate Controllers

Once the basics of MIDI are understood, other possibilities for music education can be considered. MIDI sound sources do not have to be played or controlled from a keyboard-based instrument. There are several types of wind, percussion and string control devices. Several manufacturers have produced instruments that have a system of fingering similar to that of the saxophone or recorder. Another instrument uses a set of three buttons that function like the valves on a trumpet. The student uses a wheel and buttons to select the pitch. These instruments aren't capable of producing sound themselves but can send MIDI messages to sound sources.

Percussionists have several different controller choices. Some of these devices have the look of a mallet instrument, with pads arranged in the traditional keyboard arrangement. Mallets or fingers can be used to trigger the notes. Other instruments have various-shaped pads that can be played using sticks. Each of these pads can be assigned a different percussion timbre; these instruments work well with a drum machine as the sound source. There are also arrangements of pads that are larger and have the look of a drumset. These devices are useful in sequencing drum parts, since it is frequently very difficult to produce authentic-sounding drum figures from a keyboard instrument. Some percussionists prefer to play an acoustic drumset along with a few MIDI percussion trigger pads, which they assign to synthetic gongs or unique instrumental timbres.

Violinists and cellists can make MIDI music using string-based controllers. Electronics on the fingerboard sense where the finger is placed and determine the appropriate pitch; a MIDI message is then sent to the sound source. These instruments can be bowed or plucked, or be set to respond based simply on the placement of a finger on the fingerboard.

There are MIDI players controllers based on the guitar and electric bass. Some of these units are available with their own sound sources, or they can be used to trigger any device that receives MIDI messages. These controllers have pitch-bend bars and can be played with a pick or fingers.

There are also devices that will convert musical information from an acoustic source played through a microphone and into MIDI messages. This allows flute players or singers to perform normally and produce a different timbre from a synthesizer or sampler. These *analog-to-digital converters* are improving rapidly and provide the electronic musician greater expressiveness.

These types of controllers make it possible for students with instrumental skills, other than keyboard, to become involved in using technology at a higher level. In schools, unique ensembles can be created that use alternate controllers to make music in a different way. These instruments can be adopted into traditional ensembles to add a different flavor to the overall sound.

Students can work on keyboard technique privately with the use of headphones.

Sequencer Options

Some hardware and software sequencers can synchronize to video or audiotape. This makes it possible to link digital sequences with analog audio tracks contain vocals, saxophones or strings. It is also possible to create automated mixes, in which a sequencer actually records volume changes as MIDI data can be played back later like any other MIDI message.

MIDI sequencers can even control other devices used in performance. For example, it is possible to control stage lighting through the use of MIDI messages. The brightness, color and direction of the lights can be controlled using a MIDI-to-light interface unit. If one keeps in mind that MIDI is nothing more than a series of numbers that can be translated to mean almost anything, it may not be surprising to learn that MIDI messages can be put to a variety of uses.

6

COMPUTERS

A *computer* is a device that can receive, manipulate, store and output data. A computer has no idea what the data represents or for what purpose it is being manipulated.

There are two primary components to every computer system — *hardware and software*. Hardware is the physical machine that we actually see and touch. Each computer contains CPU (central processing unit), a set of circuitry that receives and processes information and directs it to other devices such as printers, disks drives or modems. Computers also contain two kinds of memory. *ROM* (Read Only Memory) contains permanent instructions and information the computer uses to start up and update properly; these are permanent and can't be altered by the user. *RAM* (Random Access Memory) is used to store data that may need to be altered or updated. Both *applications* (word processing programs, databases, spreadsheets, etc.) and the *data files* created are in RAM.

The other component of any computer system is the set of instructions or rules the computer must follow in order to accomplish the task it is given. This set of instructions is contained in software and causes the computer to serve a particular purpose such as word processor, calculator, art sketch pad or music sequencer. Some instructions might be shared by different programs. For example, the instructions for the routines that save files might be the same for a word processor and a database.

Computers vary in several important ways. Some machines are limited in the types of work they can do because there is little software available. This is often true of new brands or models, since programmers need time to learn the capabilities of a machine and the language idiosyncrasies used in programming it. This problem may exist to a lesser degree in machines that use software originally designed for other computers. These "clones" often will run the vast majority (80-90%) of the programs available for the original computer but may be unable to run certain applications.

Processing speed is an important variable in computers. With the development of each new processing chip, the speed at which computers can process data is improved. Even within the same brand of computer a great deal of variety in speed can be found among models. Faster computers are more expensive, and the user must thus decide if the type of work being planned for the computer requires the additional speed. Graphics or image-processing applications require the computer to manipulate large amounts of data, and speed is therefore of great importance. Music notation programs are an example of applications that depend heavily on graphics; thus if a user is considering

Sequencers provide a unique opportunity for students to compose their music.

running one of these programs, he or she should also consider buying a faster computer. Word processing does not require as much speed and can usually be done satisfactorily on slower-running machines.

Memory size is another way in which computers can vary. Large amounts of memory may be required in order to run large software packages containing many instructions. There must be enough room available to store the application as well as the data created while using the application. For example, the instructions that cause the computer to act as a word processor and the individual words in a document must both be stored in the computer's memory until they are saved to some storage device. Most computer manufacturers allow for the addition of more memory through the installation of chips. This becomes important as more powerful, updated versions of software (with a greater number of instructions) become available.

Classroom Uses

The use of computers in the music classroom is limited by only the experience and vision of the classroom teacher. Classroom teachers have demonstrated a great creativity in the ways in which they've integrated computers into their instruction. Teachers will usually learn to use one type of application initially but will eventually branch out and learn to use other tools as they discover a need.

Several applications have become fairly common in music classrooms where technology is used routinely. Computers can be used to create and control sound. *Sequencing programs* allow the user to play music into the computer, store it, edit it and play it back. Many musical parameters can be altered, including tempo, timbre, key and meter, as well as the pitches of individual notes. Students can use these programs to create their own musical compositions and accompaniments. Most sequencers allow students to enter musical information from MIDI-equipped keyboards in real time or step time. These events are added one at a time until the piece is complete. These programs allow students with limited performance skills to have a creative musical experience, record their performance on cassette tape and share it at home with their families and friends.

Patch editors and *librarians* can be used to create, edit and store sounds. Patch editors are available for many different types of synthesizers. These programs allow a user to alter the various parameters of the synthesizer from the computer; they make editing easier by displaying many of the synthesizer's parameters on the screen simultaneously and in graphic form. They generally are designed to work specifically with one model of synthesizer; however, universal editors, which can edit many types of synthesizers, are becoming quite popular.

Librarian programs store the sounds of one or more synthesizers and can be organized in a couple of ways. All sounds of a certain type, for example, bass or strings, for several different synthesizers can be stored together. On the other hand, banks of sounds can be created for a particular project or for a specific synthesizer. As with editors, some of these programs are machine specific, while other, universal librarians will store patches for a variety of synthesizers and can be accessed within a sequencing program to assign sounds.

Notation software makes it possible for composers and arrangers to produce a nearly perfect musical score and parts. Notes can be entered one at a time using either a mouse or the computer keyboard. Some notation programs allow for note entry from a MIDI-equipped musical keyboard. Many of the more powerful notation programs will allow the user to import *MIDI files* created in a sequencer. This makes it possible for students to improvise melodies and accompaniments in a sequencer and then print their music out in traditional notation. No matter how scores are created, they can be edited, transposed, orchestrated and then printed on a variety of printers. These programs won't improve the quality of a student's musical ideas, but they will take much of the labor out of producing usable, readable parts. If errors are found, they can be easily detected and a new set of parts printed.

7

DRILL AND PRACTICE
SOFTWARE

Characteristics

One of the most widely used types of software in education is designed to give students the opportunity for drill and practice. These programs offer the student an opportunity to respond to questions or prompts, and provide appropriate feedback or instruction based on those responses. For certain types of educational outcomes, such as vocabulary recognition or notation identification, this is a very useful type of software. For example, students can practice identifying note names from notes displayed on a staff, or they can match musical terms with their definitions.

Synthesizer patch editing is a much simpler process when a computer is used to keep track of the various parameters.

Working with peers allows for creativity and a sense of security.

Some of these programs offer the teacher the flexibility of customizing the level of difficulty and the number of problems that must be completed successfully in order to advance to a more difficult level. This feature makes these programs more useful to a larger group of students since they can serve individuals with different levels of ability and understanding. One application might be in a classroom that has students who are mainstreamed from special programs. The software enables these students to use the same software and study the same content as the rest of the class. The teacher just sets the level so that the students can achieve success.

Evaluation

There are several considerations to be made when evaluating software for classroom use. The first is the scope of the topic considered. There are programs that focus on specific forked-fingering problems on the oboe and bassoon, while others provide instruction on rhythm, pitch, vocabulary, ear training and symbols. The teacher must decide what is needed for the instructional goal being addressed. It seems likely that a district might want to purchase broad-based programs for instruction first, then add more specific titles to their library as the need arises.

A second important consideration in software evaluation is the fit between the software and the age of the student using it. A particular piece of software might be great for third-grade students but totally wrong for high school students. Younger students seem to respond to color as part of a program. Not only is it possible that the examples might be targeted to the wrong age, but the type of reinforcement used might be totally in appropriate as well. While second-grade student might enjoy a little bear saying "nice job," a high school student might respond quite differently.

Another important consideration is the type of feedback and instruction given to the student for correct as well as incorrect responses. Obviously, "Answer Correct" and "Answer Incorrect" are not enough. Some programs provide the student with multiple opportunities to respond; when it's apparent that the student doesn't know the answer, some instruction or prompt is given.

It is possible to create a software evaluation form that considers the various questions that might influence a software choice. This could be used to compare software packages before making a purchase.

SOFTWARE REVIEW FORM

TITLE _____

PUBLISHER _____ **COST** _____

COMPUTER _____ **VERSION** _____

1. What concept(s) could be taught using this piece of software?
2. For what grade level of students is the software most appropriate?
3. What skills or knowledge would the student need to have before using this software?
4. Are there any peripheral devices needed or special memory requirements? What?
5. Is the documentation clear and understandable? How could it be improved?
6. What are the strengths of this software?
7. What are its weaknesses?
8. How could this software best be used in a music class?

One additional consideration in selecting drill and practice software might be uses for the program other than those originally intended by the author. For example, one ear-training package has a feature that allows the user to choose the key for musical examples. While choosing the key, a display is available that will play 16 different scales and modes in any key. There is a set of boxes that can be checked to indicate which notes are actually being played in the scale. This could be a very useful demonstration tool for teaching different scales and modes.

8

MANAGEMENT TOOLS

Management tools are software programs that can assist teachers in completing many of their routine record-keeping and communication tasks. These programs had their origins in the business world but can be adapted to educational record keeping and communication. Basically there are three types of tools: word processors, databases and spreadsheets. Frequently these programs are combined into a single package that allows information to be shared among programs.

Word Processors

These programs turn a computer into a sophisticated text creation, editing and production tool. Given the number of forms required each school year by music teachers, these tools are invaluable. Once created, a form or letter can be updated each year with new dates and information. Correspondence becomes easier, because form letters can be created, then simply altered to fit a particular occasion. There are powerful companion programs that make it possible to check spelling against a dictionary or to ask for a list of options from a thesaurus.

Desktop Publishing

These programs allow for the integration of word processed text, graphics and scanned images into a single document. Clip-art files of ready-made artwork are available commercially, or there are public-domain graphics accessible through telecommunication networks. These are an excellent source of ready-to-use art images. Text can be placed around spaces for pictures. The size, shape and style of the type can be altered throughout the document. Newsletters and instructional materials with a professional look can be created. Concert programs can include pictures of the band, choir, orchestra or individual students, parents or school members.

Databases

Databases are tools that allow users to determine the kind of information that will be recorded and how it will be used. Each piece of information is stored once in a location called a field. A simple student database would contain a last-name field, a first-name field, a homeroom field and a phone number field. Once the fields are created, the data for each student is entered. This information can then be sorted by the program. The list of students could be alphabetized based on the last name, or sorted by ascending or descending homeroom numbers.

Students can be sorted by name, by homeroom, or by zip code.

NAME

NAME	Homeroom	Inst	class	Address	Zip
Anitra	08	Clarinet	BAND8	2467 Weber Rd.	43211
Becky	07	Clarinet	BAND8	1551 E.N. Broadway	43232
DeShannon	211	Trumpet	BAND7	1226 Loretta	44211
Gerald	110	Alto SX	BAND7	3524 Melrose Ave.	43224
Hiawatha	08	Flute	BAND8	1954 Lakeview	43216
Jocelyn	212	Flute	BAND7	4040 Genessee	43208
Kenwanna	110	Clarinet	BAND7	3073 Pacemont	43233
Michelle	211	Flute	BAND7	360 Como	43255
Nathan	08	Trombone	BAND8	205 Tibet	43201
Todd	105	Clarinet	BAND7	1404 N. High St.	43211

Homeroom

NAME	Homeroom	Inst	class	Address	Zip
Becky	7	Clarinet	BAND8	1551 E.N. Broadway	43232
Anitra	8	Clarinet	BAND8	2467 Weber Rd.	43211
Hiawatha	8	Flute	BAND8	1954 Lakeview	43216
Nathan	8	Trombone	BAND8	205 Tibet	43201
Todd	105	Clarinet	BAND7	1404 N. High St.	43211
Gerald	110	Alto SX	BAND7	3524 Melrose Ave.	43224
Kenwanna	110	Clarinet	BAND7	3073 Pacemont	43233
DeShannon	211	Trumpet	BAND7	1226 Loretta	44211
Michelle	211	Flute	BAND7	360 Como	43255
Jocelyn	212	Flute	BAND7	4040 Genessee	43208

Zip Code

NAME	Homeroom	Inst	class	Address	Zip
Nathan	8	Trombone	BAND8	205 Tibet	43201
Jocelyn	212	Flute	BAND7	4040 Genessee	43208
Anitra	8	Clarinet	BAND8	2467 Weber Rd.	43211
Todd	105	Clarinet	BAND7	1404 N. High St.	43211
Hiawatha	8	Flute	BAND8	1954 Lakeview	43216
Gerald	110	Alto SX	BAND7	3524 Melrose Ave.	43224
Becky	7	Clarinet	BAND8	1551 E.N. Broadway	43232
Kenwanna	110	Clarinet	BAND7	3073 Pacemont	43233
Michelle	211	Flute	BAND7	360 Como	43255
DeShannon	211	Trumpet	BAND7	1226 Loretta	44211

Music libraries can be catalogued using a database. The fields might include title, composer, publisher, difficulty, key, meter, date last performed, special features, style and library number. With this system a teacher can look at all of the pieces in the library in the key of Ab major or recall the pieces performed on a spring 1987 concert.

Data can be sorted alphabetically by title:

Title

Title	Composer	FILE	LEVEL	Publisher	Key	Meter	Style
AIR	Handel	CB5	EASY	Jensen	Bb	3/4	Classical
AMERICA, THE BEAUTIFU	Ward	CB7	EASY	Alfred	Bb	4/4	Patriotic
BLUE NOTE ROCK	Feldstein	CB9	EASY	Alfred	Eb	4/4	Rock
NAVY HYMN	Lauder	CB8	EASY	Alfred	Eb	C	Hymn
RHONDO FOR FLUTES	Beethoven	CB2	DIFFICULT	Chappell	Bb	2/4	Classical
ROCK-A MY SOUL	Schaeffer	CB4	MEDIUM	Pro Art	Bb	4/4	Spiritual
ROYAL MARCH	Kinyon	CB1	EASY	Alfred	Eb	C	March
RUSSIAN PAGEANT	Rimsky-Korsakov	CB10	MEDIUM	Hal Leonard	Eb	2/4	Classical (Opera)
SILVER SCEPTER (THE)	Kinyon	CB6	EASY	Alfred	Eb	4/4	Overture
SONGS OF THE SAGE	Kinyon	CB3	EASY	Alfred	Eb	4/4	Western Medley

Data can be sorted on the basis of key:

Key

Title	Composer	FILE	LEVEL	Publisher	Key	Meter	Style
AIR	Handel	CB5	EASY	Jensen	Bb	3/4	Classical
AMERICA, THE BEAUTIFU	Ward	CB7	EASY	Alfred	Bb	4/4	Patriotic
RHONDO FOR FLUTES	Beethoven	CB2	DIFFICULT	Chappell	Bb	2/4	Classical
ROCK-A MY SOUL	Schaeffer	CB4	MEDIUM	Pro Art	Bb	4/4	Spiritual
BLUE NOTE ROCK	Feldstein	CB9	EASY	Alfred	Eb	4/4	Rock
NAVY HYMN	Lauder	CB8	EASY	Alfred	Eb	C	Hymn
ROYAL MARCH	Kinyon	CB1	EASY	Alfred	Eb	C	March
RUSSIAN PAGEANT	Rimsky-Korsakov	CB10	MEDIUM	Hal Leonard	Eb	2/4	Classical (Opera)
SILVER SCEPTER (THE)	Kinyon	CB6	EASY	Alfred	Eb	4/4	Overture
SONGS OF THE SAGE	Kinyon	CB3	EASY	Alfred	Eb	4/4	Western Medley

A list can be created based on file numbers:

Title	**Composer**	**FILE**	**LEVEL**	**Publisher**	**Key**	**Meter**	**Style**
ROYAL MARCH	Kinyon	CB1	EASY	Alfred	Eb	C	March
RHONDO FOR FLUTES	Beethoven	CB2	DIFFICULT	Chappell	Bb	2/4	Classical
SONGS OF THE SAGE	Kinyon	CB3	EASY	Alfred	Eb	4/4	Western Medley
ROCK-A MY SOUL	Schaeffer	CB4	MEDIUM	Pro Art	Bb	4/4	Spiritual
AIR	Handel	CB5	EASY	Jensen	Bb	3/4	Classical
SILVER SCEPTER (THE)	Kinyon	CB6	EASY	Alfred	Eb	4/4	Overture
AMERICA, THE BEAUTIFUL	Ward	CB7	EASY	Alfred	Bb	4/4	Patriotic
NAVY HYMN	Lauder	CB8	EASY	Alfred	Eb	C	Hymn
BLUE NOTE ROCK	Feldstein	CB9	EASY	Alfred	Eb	4/4	Rock
RUSSIAN PAGEANT	Rimsky-Korsakov	CB10	MEDIUM	Hal Leonard	Eb	2/4	Classical (Opera)

Spreadsheets

In a database, no calculation can be inside on the numbers in each of the individual cells. To do this, a spreadsheet is needed. Spreadsheets allow the user to determine what information will be displayed in a particular cell. It could be a specific number such as a dollar amount or quiz grade. It is also possible to display a calculated value; such as the balance in a checking account or the average of a series of quizzes or tests.

In order to determine the marching band "Row of the Year," one director has made use of a spreadsheet program to keep track of the points earned each week by each row. This makes the task of record keeping and reporting much easier; the calculating can be accomplished in ten minutes after each game. The total score is based on the drum majors appraisal of work through the week, an inspection before the game and the rating of a parent or other spectator from the stands. The total score is based on the drum major's appraisal of work through the week, an inspection before the game, and the rating of a parent or other spectator from the stands. The band members look forward to the new list, which is posted each Monday after a football game.

	A	B	C	D	E	F	G	H	I	J
1										
2	Row	A	B	C	F	L	K	J	R	T
3	Inspection	98	98	97	100	97	99	98	99	97
4	Game	62	62	62	77	54	75	74	72	55
5	Week	81	75	87	77	86	91	79	90	80
6	Total	241	235	246	254	237	265	251	261	232

Game #1

At the end of the season, weekly totals can be averaged to obtain an overall rating for all 10 shows. This information can be displayed as numbers in a spreadsheet.

	A	B	C	D	E	F	G	H	I	J
1										
2	ROW	A	B	C	F	L	K	S	X	T
3	GAME 1	241	235	246	254	237	265	251	261	232
4	GAME 2	265	224	246	253	249	264	238	253	243
5	GAME 3	237	203	223	224	235	231	222	243	217
6	GAME 4	259	222	242	233	256	262	234	264	245
7	GAME 5	263	228	246	239	254	261	235	269	242
8	GAME 6	338	315	314	310	319	327	310	326	314
9	GAME 7	237	186	206	201	202	216	205	238	213
10	GAME 8	238	232	252	251	260	260	247	252	252
11	GAME 9	224	200	218	205	216	230	198	210	216
12	GAME 10	233	212	211	213	123	225	210	223	204
13	11/1/90	99	100	99	99	100	92	98	97	99
14	TOTAL	2634	2357	2503	2482	2451	2633	2448	2636	2477

Title row: **ROW FINAL**

Or the same information can be displayed in a more graphic manner, such as a bar graph, which can be created by the program:

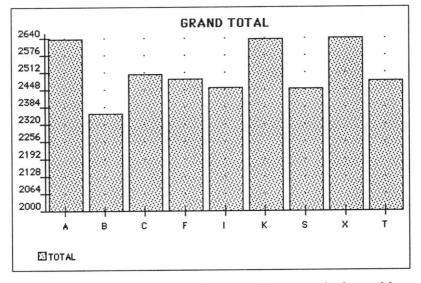

Operation of management software packages can be learned in a reasonable amount of time. They can help ease the stress felt by music teachers when they must spend too much time on record keeping, rather than rehearsing their performance groups. These packages are flexible; they can be designed to work with any number of students and will keep track of an enormous amount of data.

Band methods may include instructional software, which provides a variety of drill and practice opportunities.

9

PERIPHERAL DEVICES

Peripheral devices are pieces of equipment serving a specific purpose that can be connected to a computer. Most require software and/or special hardware interfaces (connectors) in order to function properly.

Printers have a direct effect on the quality of the final product. Dot-matrix printers are cheapest and most likely to be in a school's price range. However, laser printers are superior in quality and might be shared by several departments within a school.

Modems are used to connect computers to phone lines. This allows your computer to communicate with computers that may be separated by a great distance. Many libraries have online services available. It is possible to use a modem to access their computer and to search their catalog by title, author and subject, then check on availability of the item. A modem also allows a user to connect to bulletin board services, which might contain useful information on a variety of topics. Some of these bulletin-board services are commercial, but many are run by an individual or a small group of users with a common interest. There are commercial services available through CompuServe or Prodigy that allow you to shop or make hotel reservations through your personal computer. Most of the commercial services have a monthly fee and/or a per-minute charge to connect to the system.

Scanners make it possible to translate an image such as a photograph or graphic into a form the computer can use. There are two types of scanners. Flatbed scanners have a large scanning area on which the original image is placed face down. The scanner moves across the image and creates a digitized version of the image, which is stored in the computer as a graphics file. Hand-held scanners are smaller and more portable and can be used to scan smaller images. With either of these devices a picture could be scanned and used on the cover of a program or in a newsletter for parents.

Video cards allow the user to import video into the computer and capture individual frames as images. This makes it possible to select a frame from a videotape and save or alter it. **Video disk players, video cassette players,** and **compact disc players** can be connected to and controlled by computers. Software can allow the computer to control these devices with a great deal of precision, making it possible to control a multi-media presentation that incorporates video and audio from a variety of sources.

Classroom Uses

Modems can be used to download data files from a number of sources. Synthesizer patches, sequences, or public-domain software can be obtained using this technology. Teachers can communicate and share ideas across geography and time. Electronic-mail services allow users to send and receive messages.

Scanners can be used by students to add interest to reports and presentation. Scanned pictures can be imported into documents such as letters, musical scores or marching band charts for drills. Visual communication is gaining more attention in newspapers and magazines. Students are becoming more accustomed to the integration of pictures, charts and graphs into instructional materials. Scanners can play an important role in this process.

Scanners allow graphics to be imported into work.

Using computers to control various video and audio players, teachers and/or students can now author interesting presentations and reports that incorporate quality audio as well as a variety of visuals. Instead of being limited to the audiovisual resources available within a school district or a building, they can produce sophisticated, interesting materials in the classroom. Students can incorporate their own resources as well; sections of popular music recordings can be played followed by sections of traditional music used for instruction. These could be played while video images of the composers or performers are being displayed.

10

CURRICULUM ISSUES

Many music teachers are attempting to discover where the use of technology might fit into their curriculum. Music specialists see a gap between the current use of technology in commercial music and the stated goals of their curriculum. It is important to stress that the existing goals for music instruction have been developed over a long period of time with input from a host of professionals. These goals are still valuable, and any attempt to eliminate them should be considered very carefully. Some districts look to the state board for guidance in curriculum development. Most state curriculum guides either don't address the use of technology in the music classroom or mention it as a remote option.

Process

Frequently, the curricular integration process begins with a teacher learning enough about a specific piece of technology to use it in his or her classroom. This initial use of technology might involve creating classroom materials using a notation program or sequencing and recording listening examples. The use of P.A. systems in performances has become more common as choral directors have become more familiar with them. Initially no new curriculum goals are needed, since the teacher is only using the technology to facilitate the achievement of existing goals.

The next level of use requires that the teacher learn some new vocabulary and gain a conceptual knowledge of music technology. Since students are frequently exposed to music technology in their everyday lives, they can be an invaluable asset to the teacher in this learning process. At this level there is a curricular choice to be made. Most music curriculums contain a goal related to identifying instruments by sight, name and sound. Music technology may be integrated into this goal, or a new goal may be generated that addresses the learning of electronic instruments as a separate task.

At the highest level of instruction, students are given the skills to choose their own goals for technology. They might choose to compose their own pieces or to work on a multi-media or integrated arts project. Technology provides a powerful tool with which the students can use to experiment and create. Teachers provide expertise and give students an awareness of what is possible with the technology. They also provide feedback about musical qualities as well as how well the technology is applied. Here again there is a choice to be made concerning curricular goals. Should this creative effort be subsumed under a larger general goal of "students will have a compositional experience in the general music class," or is there a need for a new, more explicit goal? The philosophy of the district and individual teacher will provide guidance in this choice.

LEVEL of USE	TEACHER Responsibility	STUDENT Tasks
ENTRY (Teaching *WITH* Technology)	Have a working knowledge of specifically needed technology.	Respond to the materials and examples created by the teacher.
COGNITIVE (Teaching *ABOUT* technology)	Be able to identify equipment by name and function.	Learn about the technology being used to produce music.
INDEPENDENT (Teaching *TO USE* technology)	Demonstrate and provide feedback. Help solve technical problems.	Choose goals for the use of technology. Create product. Evaluate product. Learn processes/ procedures. Solve problems.

11

GRANTSMANSHIP

Why?

One of the obvious consequences of deciding to integrate technology into an existing educational setting is the emergence of a substantial and ongoing need for funding. Fund-raising has become a standard activity in most music programs, and the annual candy, fruit, or pizza sale is a steady source of income. However, considering the expense of technology and the fact that it is not a mainstay of the basic music program, alternative sources of funding can be considered.

How to Apply

The key to any successful grant application is the quality of the idea on which the application is based. If you haven't a clue as to the purpose or use of technology in the classroom, and it appears that your only motivation for obtaining this grant is to purchase equipment for an unclear objective, then your chances of being funded are reduced. Most funding agencies have only a small grants budget, and they want to feel secure that money is being used in a responsible and productive way. The clarity and importance of your idea will provide them with this security.

First, consider the total music program and identify those objectives that are not being fulfilled or instructional experiences that are difficult to provide. Next, consider the role technology could play in the instructional process to provide a more complete music education for the students. In answering these questions, the basic purpose or idea for the grant will become clearer.

Although each grant-funding agency will have different application procedures and/or forms, there will be remarkable consistency concerning the type of information they desire. Several of the most common components include:

Cover Letter/summary

This is crucial since it may serve as the initial screening for the entire application. The reader should be "hooked" by this section. After reading this section, the reader should know who you are, what students you work with, what your goal is and how this grant can help to achieve this goal.

Introduction

This section contains further information about the applicant and contributes to a secure feeling for the grant-funding agency in knowing who they are trusting with their funds. Include your education, experience and relevant accomplishments. Listing any prior grants that were refunded might be useful here, especially if you are applying for funds to move forward in developing a more comprehensive program.

Statement of the Problem

What problem have you identified within your own program? What experience is lacking for your students? What curricular goal is being ignored? Create an understanding of the importance of the need for your program. Tie this to existing curricular goals, if possible. In some cases it makes sense to use numbers (percentages, number of students served or participating, etc.) to document a need. This use of numbers can also serve as the basis of an objective or goal.

Goals or Objectives

Once the need has been identified, then a clear, measurable objective for satisfying that need should be written. Try to be as specific as possible. Make use of numbers to document improvement. Whatever your goal, make sure that the reader (even a nonmusician) understands what your ultimate outcome will be.

Method or Procedure

The reader should be provided an understanding of the steps involved in completing the project. What will the schedule be? How long will this project last? Who will be trained? Who will be responsible for the various parts of the project? Where will the project take place? This should be a recipe for how the project will be accomplished. Given similar circumstances, another music teacher should be able to take this recipe and produce similar results.

Evaluation

Obviously, if someone is willing to provide funds for a project, they'll want to know if their money actually was of benefit. A comprehensive evaluation procedure will serve this purpose. Include information concerning who will do the evaluation, when will it be done, and how the results will be shared with other teachers, as well as the community at large. Once again, if the results can include a score or number, it will be easier for some readers to understand. This number may be only one type of reported outcome along with a descriptive statement of the feelings or attitudes of the students.

Budget

Ask for a specific dollar amount and ask for the total amount you actually need to complete the project. If you ask for more than you need, you'll have difficulty justifying the amount. If you decide to ask for less than you really need, then you'll fail to accomplish your objective. It seems better to be rejected for requesting what you really need than to receive too little money to succeed in accomplishing your goal.

Notation programs allow students to create and print their own music scores.

Grantwriting is a skill that can be learned and improved through practice. The fact that a particular source might not fund your project may have nothing to do with the quality of the idea on which the project was based. If you feel that the idea has merit, then submit it to another agency. Don't wait to celebrate until you receive the funds. Celebrate when the form is completed and submitted.

Where to Apply

Although there are many demands on the funds of local schools and school districts, don't overlook these sources. Don't forget the PTA/O, the general fund of the school, and/or state and federal money available to the district.

There is a traditional bond between community-service organizations and the schools. Kiwanis, Lions, Optimist, and Rotary clubs all exist to improve their communities. There are several important considerations in submitting grantfunding requests to these organizations.

1. Most service clubs are made up of men and women who are not musicians or teachers. They are reasonable people who will be supportive of reasonable requests if it is possible. It may be necessary to educate these groups about the process of teaching and learning in music before they can consider your request.

2. Service clubs operate on limited budgets and need to get the maximum exposure and public recognition for their contributions. Pictures of the club officers with technology and children are very useful to these groups, since they must document their community services to state or national offices.

3. If money has already been raised toward a project, include the amount in the request. This demonstrates a commitment on the part of the music program to this project. Also, name other sources of support that have been contacted.

The most difficult part of grant writing is identifying those agencies and organizations that actually fund educational grants in a particular area. Most school districts have a person who is responsible for writing large grants and who could be of assistance in identifying local funding sources. If there is no such person, contact local arts councils or other nonprofit organizations. Even if these initial contacts don't work out, they may provide leads for others that will. Frequently colleges and universities will have entire offices dedicated to grants. Don't hesitate to enlist their help in identifying sources. Professional journals frequently advertise contests, grants and other sources of funding. If you're applying for money to fund technology in music, don't limit your search to music grants. Consider the various grants that fund research into the use of technology in education.

It has always been important for the music specialist to accept the role of expert in matters of music instruction in their own district. With the introduction of technology into music education, this is more true now than ever before. Teachers must remain current about what is possible and available by reading professional literature and attending conventions and workshops. After gaining an understanding of the possibilities, it is up to the individual teacher to select from the options the specific items most appropriate for his or her own classroom. The music education specialist is the *best* person to make these decisions. The technology specialist may be of assistance in answering questions concerning the capabilities of equipment, but he or she is not trained as a musician and should not make decisions concerning the application of technology to music education.

GLOSSARY

-A-

A/D converter   a device that translates analog information into digital information, which a computer can process and store.

Additive Synthesis   the addition of several simple, independent waves to create a more complex sound.

ADSR   attack, decay, sustain, and release; elements of the envelope, which describes the way a sound changes over time.

Aftertouch   a feature found on some synthesizer keyboards in which key pressure can produce MIDI messages. These messages can control the brightness of a particular timbre or introduce vibrato into the sound.

Algorithm   a set design of instructions followed to arrive at some conclusion.

Amplifier   a device used to increase the amplitude or strength of a signal. Audio amplifiers boost audio signals.

Analog   continuous output with no gaps between values. Contrast with digital, which is not continuous but rather a series of numbers that represent the state of the signal at different points. A violin is an analog instrument. A sampled violin sound would be a digital representation of that sound.

Attack   the beginning of a sound. A gong has a slow attack, while a snare drum has a fast attack.

Autocorrect   see quantization.

-B-

Bandwidth

the range of frequencies which can be generated or processed.

Bank

a group of patches (timbres) that can be loaded as a group into the memory of a synthesizer.

Basic Channel

the MIDI channel used to transmit messages to and from different devices.

Baud

commonly used as a standard for how many bits of information are able to be transmitted in one second. MIDI devices transmit information at a rate of 32,000 baud (bits per second).

Bit

binary digit, or single piece of digital information.

Breath Controller

a device that generates MIDI information based on a player's breath pressure and fingering patterns. Frequently has a key arrangement similar to an acoustic wind instrument such as a trumpet or saxophone.

Byte

a set of eight or more bits. Used to transmit a single character or letter.

-C-

CD-ROM

a "read only" storage device which can contain up to 660,000,000 bytes of storage. Encyclopedias are available in this format.

Channel

in MIDI one of the 16 available routes for information to travel. Each MIDI device can be set to receive or transmit on any of the 16 channels; communication is only possible between devices that share a common send/receive channel.

Channel Messages

MIDI messages to a particular channel.

Channelize

assigning MIDI data to a particular channel.

Click Track

a pulse provided by an electronic source sequencer that acts as a metronome.

Clock	the timing reference used by an entire MIDI system. Devices that generate clock timing (such as drum machines) can usually act as the system master (responding to internal clock) or as a slave unit (responding to external clock).
Computer	an electronic device which receives, processes, stores and outputs information.
Controller	any device used to operate a synthesizer. Can be a separate device, such as a wind, string or drum controller, or can actually be part of the synthesizer, such as a keyboard or pitch-bend wheel.
Cut	to remove information from a file.
Cut and Paste	to remove information from a location in a file and place somewhere else in the file or in a different file.

-D-

DAT	digital audio tape. Digital audio tape recorders make use of digital technology to produce recordings similar in quality to that of compact discs.
Data	individual pieces or groups of information processed by a computer.
Decrement	to decrease the value of a number along some scale of set values.
Database	a type of software program that allows the user to define different types of information and then organize that information in different ways depending on the user's needs.
Disk	a magnetic storage medium for storing computer data. Floppy disks are commony available in 5.25- and 3.5-inch formats.
Disk Drive	the device that reads the information stored on a disk and transfers it into the CPU for processing.
Dot Matrix	a type of printer in which the letters are formed on the basis of a grid. Similar to creating letters by darkening in squares of graph paper.

Drill and Practice   software that provides examples and opportunities for students to respond to those examples. Feedback is then provided based on these responses.

Drum Controller   a pad or set of pads that, when struck, generates MIDI data instead of percussion sounds.

Duration   the length of a musical event. May be expressed as a musical rhythmic value or in numerical form.

-E-

Effect   an alteration of the original sound. Often used to create the illusion of an acoustic environment in a synthetic situation. Common effects include reverb, chorusing, and detuning.

Emulate   to imitate another device. A computer sequencing program will often have transport controls that emulate those of a multitrack tape recorder.

Enable   turn on a function.

Envelope   see ADSR.

Equalization   the process of boosting (increasing) or cutting (decreasing) the relative strength of particular frequencies. This process will alter a sound's timbre and may make it more or less prominent in the final mix.

-F-

Fader   a volume control on a mixer.

File   a collection of data which has some common element. A word processor file may be focused on a topic or a music sequencer file may contain a single piece of music.

Filter   a device which restricts the flow of data. Used to cut certain audio frequencies.

Frequency   the number of cycles per second expressed in Hertz. The range of human hearing is frequently expressed as 20Hz to 20,000 Hz.

-G-

Gain
refers to the amount of amplication. Increasing the gain increases the level of amplification.

Glitch
a problem with the operation of a piece of hardware or software.

Graphic
refers to the use of pictures or icons to represent programs, data, or controls instead of numbers.

Guitar Controller
a device having the appearance of a guitar that can transmit data and control MIDI equipment.

-H-

Hard Copy
a printed copy. A score printed on paper is a hard copy of the data displayed on the computer screen when using a notation program.

Hard Disk
a storage device used to store large amounts of data on a large, rigid magnetic surface.

Hard Disk Recording
direct storage of digital audio information to a hard disk. This data can be saved, processed, and edited.

Hardware
the physical pieces of equipment that make up a system.

Hertz
cycles per second.

Highpass Filter
a filter used to restrict the presence of low frequencies. This filter allows high frequencies to pass through.

-I-

Icon
a graphic representation of a file or application which can be used to select that file or application.

IMA
International MIDI Association

Increment
to increase the value of a number along some scale of set values.

Interface	a device that allows two or more pieces of equipment to communicate.
I/O	input/output.

-J-

Jack	the female half of a connecting pair. The plug is connected into the jack.

-K-

k	kilo, meaning 1,000. A frequency of 14kHz would be 14,000 cycles per second.
Keyboard Controller	a device used to transmit data and control MIDI equipment that has the appearance of a keyboard instrument.
Keyboard Split	a feature on some synthesizers that allows the keyboard to be divided and generate different MIDI data from each area of the keyboard. This "splitting" of the keyboard allows, for example, notes below middle C to produce bass sounds while those above middle C produce piano sounds .
Key Disk	some computer software requires that the user have an original disk from the manufacturer in order to start up the program. This original disk is called the key disk.

-L-

Laser Printer	a printer that produces better definition of the characters and figures and is used to produce higher quality output than a dot matrix printer.
Librarian	a type of software that allows for the storage and organization of sounds for synthesizers.

Local Control　　a feature on some keyboard instruments that allows the user to separate the keyboard from the sound producing unit of the instrument. This makes it possible to use the keyboard as a controller without triggering the sounds within the instrument.

Loop　　a feature on some sequencers that allows a pattern or section to be repeated or recorded. For example, a drum pattern may be repeated several times. Instead of recording it over and over, it can be recorded once and then looped for the additional repetitions.

Lowpass Filter　　a filter used to restrict the presence of high frequencies. This filter allows low frequencies to pass through.

-M-

Master Volume　　the final control of dynamic level in a mixer or recorder.

Megabyte　　1,048,576 bytes of information. A 20MB hard drive would hold 20 x 1,048,576 or 20,971,520 bytes of information.

Memory　　storage locations for data in a computer.

Memory Protect　　a feature that makes it impossible to alter a voice or parameter in a synthesizer until the protection is turned off.

Message　　either an instruction or some value transmitted between devices.

MIDI　　Musical Instrument Digital Interface

MMA　　MIDI Manufacturers Association.

Modem　　a device that allows for communication between computers across phone lines.

Modulation Wheel　　one of the control devices commonly found on synthesizers. Can be used to alter modulation or can be assigned to control some other aspect of sound.

Multitimbral   capable of producing multiple sounds simultaneously.

-N-

NAMM   National Association of Music Merchants

Noise Gate   a device which takes in audio signals and filters out those that are weaker than the level set by the user. This device is used to filter out noise and only allow music through.

Note ON/OFF   a MIDI message that causes notes to start and stop.

-O-

Omni MODE   MIDI mode that, when enabled, allows the device to respond to messages coming in from any of the sixteen different MIDI channels.

Operator   the basis of FM synthesis. The operator generates the carrier and modulation waves.

Optical Storage   mass read/write storage devices that are based on patterns of light rather than on magnetism.

Oscillator   the part of a synthesis system that generates the waves forms.

Overdub   after the first track has been recorded on a multi-track tape recording or a sequencer, each additional track is an overdub.

-P-

Pan Pot   the control on a mixing console that allows the user to position the audio signal across the left-to-right stereo spectrum.

Patch
synthesizer timbre. In early synthesizers, several patch cords were used to route the sound to the various components of the synthesizer. A particular configuration of patch cords was called a patch.

Patch Editor
a type of software used to edit synthesizer voices that displays the various parameters and their values. These programs are available for specific synthesizers, or some have a broader application to several keyboards.

Pitch Bend Wheel
one of the control devices commonly found on synthesizers. Can be used to shift pitch either up or down or can be assigned to control some other aspect of sound.

Polyphonic
capable of sounding more than one note simultaneously.

Portamento
an effect in synthesizers that refers to sliding between notes.

Preset
sounds housed in synthesizer memory and easily accessible.

Program
(1) a set of instructions for a computer or (2) a particular sound in a synthesizer (patch).

Program Change
a MIDI message that recalls a specific sound by number from the sound banks available in a synthesizer.

$-Q_{\sim}$

Quantization
a feature of sequencers and drum machines that rounds off all of the rhythmic values to the nearest defined value. For example, after sequencing a track a user can move the notes forward or back until they all line up with a given note value, such as a sixteenth note.

-R-

RAM

Randon Access Memory stores data within the computer. RAM is volatile memory in that it can be erased if the electricity to the computer is turned off.

RAM Cartridge

used to store sounds and files for a synthesizer on a cartridge or card. Can load sounds quickly.

Read

process of transferring data from some storage device into computer memory.

ROM

Read Only Memory cannot be changed. Data in ROM can only be read, not written as in RAM.

-S-

Sample

a digitized sound saved into a computer or sampling keyboard.

Sample Length

how long the sample lasts. Depends on the memory capabilities of the sampling device.

Sample Rate

how often the original sound is sampled and a digital representation stored.

Sampler

a device designed to digitally record, edit and play back sounds.

Save

a command used to instruct the computer to store data to a device such as a floppy disk, or hard disk drive.

SCSI

Small Computer System Interface (skuzzy) is a system for transferring large amounts of data between computers and other devices. Can be used to download samples into a sampler from a computer.

Sequence

a piece of music stored as a set of MIDI messages.

Sequencer

a device that can record, edit and play back sequences.

Software

a set of instructions for a computer to follow.

Spreadsheet

a type of software program that allows for the organization and manipulation of numbers. Used for accounting and management.

Sustain Pedal one of the control devices commonly found on synthesizers. Can be used to alter the length of notes or can be assigned to control some other aspect of sound.

-T-

Thru Box a device used to pass through MIDI information to multiple devices simultaneously instead of daisy chaining. This eliminates the possibility of delay as the signal is passed from one device to the next.

Timbre characteristic or identifiable sound.

Touch-Sensitivity the ability of MIDI devices to generate or respond to the velocity with which a key is struck.

Track contains discrete independent musical information either on audio tape or in a sequence.

-U-

Unison mode in which all of the voices of a synthesizer are set to play the same timbre with the same tuning.

Upload to send data from a computer to some other location. Frequently used to describe the transferring of files to bulletin boards or user groups via a modem.

User Interface the hardware, displays, and controls used to interact with a computer or synthesizer.

-V-

VCA Voltage Controlled Amplifier increases the strength of a signal as additional voltage is applied.

VCF Voltage Controlled Filter controls the frequencies that are allowed to pass through the system as voltage is applied.

VCO	Voltage Controlled Oscillator generates sound waves and varies the frequency as voltage is applied.
Velocity	the speed of the key as it is depressed on a keyboard. The time it takes to move from the key-up position to the key-down position.

-W-

Word Processor	a type of software that allows the user to create, edit, and print documents.

-X Y Z-

Zone	**a range** of keys on a keyboard. Can be assigned a specific timbre or sample.

REFERENCES

Because it is extremely difficult to cite every possible resource, this list represents the *kinds* of resources that are available. In addition to these resources, manufacturers often publish and distribute information. Roland, for example, publishes a users' group magazine. It is very likely that there are other titles that you might want to consider. Request catalogs from the publishers for other sources.

Magazines

Electronic Musician
Keyboard
Musician
The Music and Computer Educator

Books

Casabona, Helen, and David Frederick. *Using MIDI*, Cupertino, Calif.: GPI Publications, 1987.

Casabona, Helen; and David Frederick and Tom Darter. *Beginning Synthesizer*, Cupertino, Calif.: GPI Publications, 1986.

Chamberlin Hal. *Musical Applications of Microprocessors, 1987.*

De Furia, Steve. *The Secrets of Analog and Digital Synthesis*, Rutherford, N.J.: Third Earth Publishing, Inc., 1986.

De Furia, Steve and Joe Scacciaferro. *The MIDI Book*, Third Pomton Lakes, N.J.: Earth Publishing Inc., 1987.

De Furia, Steve and Joe Scacciaferro. *The MIDI Implementation Book*, Pomton Lakes, N.J.: Third Earth Publishing, Inc., 1987.

De Furia, Steve and Joe Scacciaferro. *The MIDI Resource Book*, Pomton Lakes, N.J.: Third Earth Publishing Inc., 1987.

De Furia, Steve and Joe Scacciaferro. *The SAMPLING Book*, Pomton Lakes, N.J.: Third Earth Publishing Inc., 1987.

De Furia, Steve and Joe Scacciaferro. *The MIDI System Exclusive Book*, Pomton Lakes, N.J.: Third Earth Publishing Inc., 1987.

Deutsch, Herbert A. *Synthesis An Introduction to the History, Theory, & Practice of Electronic Music*, Van Nuys, Calif: Alfred Publishing Co. Inc., 1985.

Eiche, Jon F. *What's a Synthesizer?*, Milwaukee, Wisc.: Hal Leonard Books, 1987.

Friedman, Dean. *The Complete Guide to Synthesizers, Sequencers, & Drum Machines*, New York, N.Y.: Amsco Publications, 1985.

Massey, Howard. *The Complete Guide to MIDI Software*, New York, N.Y.: Amsco Publications, 1986.

Milano, Dominic, ed. *Mind Over MIDI*, Cupertino, Calif.: GPI Publications, 1987.

Milano, Dominic, ed. *Synthesizer Progamming*, Cupertino, Calif.: GPI Publications, 1987.

Moog, Bob; Roger Powell; Tom Rhea; and Steve Porcaro. *Synthesizer Basics*, Cupertino, Calif.: GPI Publications, 1984.

Moog, Bob; Roger Powell; and Craig Anderton. *Synthesizers and Computers*, Cupertino, Calif.: GPI Publications, 1985.

Otsuka, Akiro & Akihiko Nakajima. *MIDI BASICS*, New York, N.Y.: Amsco Publishing Co., 1987.

Rona, Jeff. *MIDI, Ins, Outs, & Thrus*, Milwaukee, Wisc.: Hal Leonard Books, 1987.

Rothstein, Joseph. *MIDI: A Comprehensive Introduction*, Madison, Wisc.: A-R Editions, 1991.

Rudolph, Thomas E. *Music and the Apple II*, Drexell Hill, Penn.: Unsinn Publications, 1984.

Walker, Dan. *1990 How MIDI Works*, Newbury Park, Calif.: Alexander Publishing, 1990.

Software

Composition

Ludwig
(Atari)
Hybrid Arts
8522 National Blvd.
Los Angeles, CA 90232

Pop-Tune
(IBM)
AD LIB
50 Stanford St.
Boston, MA 02114

Personal Composer
(IBM)
MEI
PO Box 599
328 E-l 1300 North
Chesterton, IN 46304

Visual Composer
(IBM)
AD LIB
50 Stanford St.
Boston, MA 02114

Digital Audio

Sound Tools
(IBM)
Digidesign
1360 Willow Rd.
Menlo Park, CA 94025

Digital Recording

SoundStage
(IBM)
Turtle Beach
PO Box 5074
York, PA 17405

Studio Vision
(Macintosh)
Opcode
3641 Haven Dr. Ste. A
Menlo Park, CA 94025-1010

Digital Sampler

SampleCell
(Macintosh)
Digidesign
1360 Willow Rd. # 101
Menlo Park, CA 94025

Editor

Gen Edit
(Atari / Macintosh)
Hybrid Arts
8522 National Blvd.
Los Angeles, CA 90232

SAMPLEMAKER
(Atari)
Dr.T s
100 Crescent Rd.
Needham, MA 02194

Tiger Cub
(Amiga / Atari)
Dr.T's
100 Crescent Rd.
Needham, MA 02194

Editor/Librarians

Alchemy
(Macintosh)
Passport Designs
625 Miramontes
Half Moon Bay, CA 94019

Bartleby Editor \ Librarian
(IBM)
Bartleby
P.O. Box 671112
Dallas, TX 75367

Caged Artist
(Amiga / Atari / Macintosh)
Dr.T's
100 Crescent Rd.
Needham, MA 02194

Galaxy
(Macintosh)
Opcode
3641 Haven Dr. Ste. A
Menlo Park, CA 94025-1010

MIDI Quest
(Amiga / Atari / IBM /
Macintosh)
Sound Quest
66 Broadway Ave. Suite 1207
Toronto, ON, Canada
M4P 2T4

Sample Vision
(IBM)
Turtle Beach
PO Box 5074
York, PA 17405D

Softsynth
(Atari / Macintosh)
Digidesign
1360 Willow Rd. Ste. 101
Menlo Park, CA 94025

Sound Designer II
(Macintosh)
Digidesign
1360 Willow Rd. Ste. 101
Menlo Park, CA 94025

Turbosynth
(Macintosh)
Digidesign
1360 Willow Rd .
Menlo Park, CA 94025

Education

Adult Piano Theory Software
(Atari / Commodore / IBM /
Macintosh)
Alfred
PO Box 10003
Van Nuys, CA 91410-0003

**AudioGraphic Dictionary of
Harmony**
(Macintosh)
TEACHNOLOGY
11220 W. Florrisant, Suite 303
St. Louis, MO 63033

Chord Magic
(Atari / IBM / Macintosh)
Digital Horizons
PO Box 956
Welches, OR 97067

Harmony Grid
(Macintosh)
Hip Software
117 Harvard St.
Cambridge, MA 02139

Jazz Improvisation Series
(Apple IIe / Atari / IBM /
Macintosh)
ECS
1210 Lacaster Dr.
Champaign, IL 61821

Keyboard Blues
(Apple IIe / Atari / IBM /
Macintosh)
ECS
1210 Lacaster Dr.
Champaign, IL 61821

**Keyboard Extended Jazz
Harmonies**
(Apple IIe / Atari / IBM /
Macintosh)
ECS
1210 Lacaster Dr.
Champaign, IL 61821

Keyboard Jazz Harmonies
(Apple IIe / Atari / IBM /
Macintosh)
ECS
1210 Lacaster Dr.
Champaign, IL 61821

Keyboard Kapers
(Apple IIe / Atari / IBM /
Macintosh)
ECS
1210 Lacaster Dr.
Champaign, IL 61821

Keyboard Note Drill
(Apple IIe / Atari)
ECS
1210 Lacaster Dr.
Champaign, IL 61821

Listen
(Macintosh)
CTM
1013 S. Claremont Ste. 1
San Mateo, CA 94402

Maestro Music Drills
(Apple II)
Maestro Music
2403 San Mateo NE,
Suite P-12
Albuquerque, NM 87110

Maestroscope Music Theory
(Apple II)
Maestro Music
2403 San Mateo NE, Suite P- 12
Albuquerque, NM 87110

Maestroscope Theory Readiness
(Apple II)
Maestro Music
2403 San Mateo NE, Suite P-12
Albuquerque, NM 87110

MiBAC MUSIC LESSONS
(Macintosh)
MiBAC
P.O. Box 468
Northfield, MN 55057

MicroNotes Music Theory
(Apple IIe Apple IIGS)
TEACHNOLOGY
11220 W. Florrisant, Suite 303
St. Louis, MO 63033

Music Machine
(IBM)
Voyetra
333 5th Ave.
Pelham, NY 10803

MusicShapes
(Apple IIGS)
Music Systems For Learning
76 Davenport Road
Roxbury, CT 06783

Note Wizard
(Atari / IBM / Macintosh)
Digital Horizons
PO Box 956
Welches, OR 97067

Perceive
(Macintosh)
Coda
1401 East 79th St.
Bloomington, MN 55425

Piano Partners
(IBM)
MEI
PO Box 599
328 E-l 1300 North
Chesterton, IN 46304

Piano Theory Software
(Atari / Commodore / IBM /
Macintosh)
Alfred
PO Box 10003
Van Nuys, CA 91410-0003

Play It By Ear
(IBM)
IBIS Software
90 New Montgomery Street
Suite 820
San Francisco, CA 94105

Playbacks Ear Training
(IBM)
MEI
PO Box 599
328 E-l 1300 North
Chesterton, IN 46304

Practica Musica
(Macintosh)
Ars Nova
PO Box 637
Kirkland, WA 98083

Practical Theory
(Atari / Commodore / IBM
Macintosh)
Alfred
PO Box 10003
Van Nuys, CA 91410-0003

Pyware Ear Trainer
(Apple IIe)
PYGRAPHICS
PO Box 639
Grapevine, TX 76051

Rhythm Reading
(Apple II)
Maestro Music
2403 San Mateo NE,
Suite P-12
Albuquerque, NM 87110

Rhythm Time
(Atari / IBM / Macintosh)
Digital Horizons
PO Box 956
Welches, OR 97067

RhythmAce
(IBM)
IBIS Software
90 New Montgomery Street,
Suite 820
San Francisco, CA 94105

Swan Tutorials
(Apple II / Commodore / IBM)
MEI
PO Box 599
328 E-l 1300 North
Chesterton, IN 46304

Film Scoring

Cue
(Macintosh)
Opcode
3641 Haven Dr. Ste. A
Menlo Park, CA 94025-1010

Film Composer's Time Processor
(IBM)
AURICLE CONTROL SYTEMS
3828 Woodcliff Rd.
Sherman Oaks, CA 91403

Q Sheet
(Macintosh)
Digidesign
1360 Willow Rd. Ste. 101
Menlo Park, CA 94025

Interactive Composition

Bender/MCTV
(IBM)
LTA Production
PO Box 6623
Hamden, CT 06517

Drummer
(IBM)
Cool Shoes
PO Box 391
Burlington, MA 01803

Jam Factory
(Macintosh)
Dr. T's
100 Crescent Rd.
Needham, MA 02194

M
(Amiga / IBM)
Dr. T's
100 Crescent Rd.
Needham, MA 02194

MacDrums
(Macintosh)
Coda
1401 East 79th St.
Bloomington, MN 55425

Masterpiece
(Atari)
Digital Horizons
PO Box 956
Welches, OR 97067

Music Mouse
(Amiga / Atari / Macintosh)
Dr. T's
100 Crescent Rd.
Needham, MA 02194

Ovaltune
(Macintosh)
Dr. T's
100 Crescent Rd.
Needham, MA 02194

Sound Globs
(IBM)
Cool Shoes
PO Box 391
Burlington, MA 01803

TrackGenie
(IBM)
LTA Production
PO Box 6623
Hamden, CT 06517

UpBeat
(Macintosh)
Dr. T's
100 Crescent Rd.
Needham, MA 02194

Management

Pyware Music Administrator
  (Apple IIe / Apple IIGS / IBM)
  PYGRAPHICS
  PO Box 639
  Grapevine, TX 76051

Marching Band

**Multi-Dimensional MB Show
Design**
  (IBM)
  MEI
  PO Box 599 328 E-l 1300 North
  Chesterton, IN 46304

Pyware Charting Aid
  (Apple IIe / Apple IIGS / IBM)
  PYGRAPHICS
  PO Box 639
  Grapevine, TX 76051

Pyware Deluxe Charting Aid
  (Apple IIGS)
  PYGRAPHICS
  PO Box 639
  Grapevine, TX 76051

Multi-Media

Audiomedia
  (IBM / Macintosh)
  Digidesign
  1360 Willow Rd.
  Menlo Park, CA 94025

Notation

Copyist
  (Amiga / IBM)
  Dr. T's
  100 Crescent Rd.
  Needham, MA 02194

DynaDuet
  (IBM)
  Dynaware
  1163 Chess Drive, Suite J
  Foster City, CA 94404

Encore
  (IBM / Macintosh)
  Passport Designs
  625 Miramontes
  Half Moon Bay, CA 94019

Erato Software Manuscriptor
  (IBM / Automix)
  Erato Software
  P.O. Box 6278
  Salt Lake City, UT 84152-6278

FINALE
  (IBM)
  Coda
  1401 79th St.
  Minneapolis, MN 55425

Laser Music Processor
  (IBM)
  TEACH Services
  182 Donlvan Rd.
  Brushton, NY 12916

Music Printer Plus
  (IBM)
  Temporal Acuity
  300-120th Ave.
  Bellevue, WA 98005

Music Prose
  (Macintosh)
  Coda
  1401 79th St.
  Minneapolis, MN 55425

Musicad
  (IBM)
  Music Software
  Suite 111,1105 Chicago Ave
  Oak Park, IL 60302

Notator
  (Atari)
  C-Lab
  130 9th Street #303
  San Francisco, CA 94103

Noteprocessor
  (IBM)
  Thought Processors
  584 Bergen St.
  Brooklyn, NY 11238

NoteWriter II
(Macintosh)
Passport Designs
625 Miramontes
Half Moon Bay, CA 94019

Professional Composer
(Macintosh)
Mark of the Unicorn
222 Third Street
Cambridge, MA 02142

Pyware Music Writer
(Apple IIe / Apple IIGS / IBM/
Macintosh)
PYGRAPHICS
PO Box 639
Grapevine, TX 76051

SCORE 3
(IBM)
Passport Designs
625 Miramontes
Half Moon Bay, CA 94019

Theme, The Music Editor
(IBM)
THEME SOFTWARE
PO Box 8204
Charlottsville, VA 22906

Rhythm Composition

FWAP!
(IBM)
LTA Production
PO Box 6623
Hamden, CT 06517

Sequencing

Automix
(Amiga)
Dr. T's
100 Crescent Rd.
Needham, MA 02194

Ballade
(IBM)
DYNAWARE
950 Tower Lane
Foster City, CA 94404

Beyond
(Macintosh)
Dr. T's
100 Crescent Rd.
Needham, MA 02194

Cadenza
(IBM)
Big Noise
PO Box 23740
Jacksonville, FL 32241

Cakewalk
(IBM)
Twelve Tone Systems
PO Box 760
Watertown, MA 02272

Creator
(Atari)
C-Lab
130 9th Street #303
San Francisco, CA 94103

Diversi-Tune
(IIgs)
Diversified
34880 Bunker Hill
Farmington, MI 48331-3236

Edit Track II
(Atari)
Hybrid Arts
8522 National Blvd.
Los Angeles, CA 90232

EZ Score Plus
(Atari)
Hybrid Arts
8522 National Blvd.
Los Angeles, CA 90232

EZ Vision
(Macintosh)
Opcode
3641 Haven Dr. Ste. A
Menlo Park, CA 94025-1010

Final Cut
(Atari / IBM)
Digital Horizons
PO Box 956
Welches, OR 97067

Forte I
(IBM)
LTA Production
PO Box 6623
Hamden, CT 06517

Forte II
(IBM)
LTA Production
PO Box 6623
Hamden, CT 06517

KCS
(Amiga)
Dr. T's
100 Crescent Rd.
Needham, MA 02194

LEVEL II
(Amiga / IBM / Macintosh)
Dr. T's
100 Crescent Rd.
Needham, MA 02194

Master Tracks Jr.
(Atari / IBM / Macintosh)
Passport Designs
625 Miramontes
Half Moon Bay, CA 94019

Master Tracks Pro
(Amiga / Atari / IBM /
Macintosh)
Passport Designs
625 Miramontes
Half MoonBay, CA 94019

MIDI RECORDING STUDIO
(Amiga / Atari)
Dr. T's
100 Crescent Rd.
Needham, MA 02194

MIDISoft Studio
(IBM)
MIDISOFT
PO Box 1000
Bellevue, WA 98009

Prism
(IBM)
Magnetic Music
6 Twin Rocks Rd.
Brookfield, CT 06804-6909

Professional Performer
(Macintosh)
Mark of the Unicorn
222 Third Street
Cambridge, MA 02142

Real - Time
(Atari)
Dr. T's
100 Crescent Rd.
Needham, MA 02194

Rhapsody
(Macintosh)
Green Oak
4446 Salisbury Dr.
Carlsland, CA 92008

Sequencer Plus
(IBM)
Voyetra
333 5th Ave.
Pelham, NY 10803

SMPTE Track
(Atari)
Hybrid Arts
8522 National Blvd.
Los Angeles, CA 90232

Sound Exciter
(Macintosh)
Passport Designs
625 Miramontes
Half Moon Bay, CA 94019

Texture
(IBM)
Magnetic Music
6 Twin Rocks Rd.
Brookfield, CT 06804-6909

Tiger
(Amiga / Atari)
Dr.T's
100 Crescent Rd.
Needham, MA 02194

TRAX
(Amiga / Atari / IBM /
Macintosh)
Passport Designs
625 Miramontes
Half MoonBay, CA 94019

Vision
(Macintosh)
Opcode
3641 Haven Dr. Ste. A
Menlo Park, CA 94025-1010

Sound Design

Pyware Instrument Designer
(Apple IIGS)
PYGRAPHICS
PO Box 639
Grapevine, TX 76051

Synthesis

Instrument Maker
(IBM)
AD LIB
50 Stanford St.
Boston, MA 02114

Uniform Inventory

Unipro
(IBM)
MEI
PO Box 599
328 E-1 1300 North
Chesterton, IN 46304